S0-BNQ-318

Angel Island

by Wallis Campbell

Text copyright © 2007 by Mondo Publishing

Photography and Illustration Credits:

Every effort has been made to trace the ownership of all copyright materials
in this book and to obtain permission for their use.

Cover, pp 2-3: © Igor Polk, http://www.virtuar.com; p. 1: © Catherine Karnow/CORBIS; p. 5 (large map): Courtesy
of the University of Texas Libraries, The University of Texas as Austin; p. 5 (inset map): Courtesy
bayinsider.ktvu.com; p. 6 (top): © North Wind/Nancy Carter/North Wind Picture Archives; p. 6 (bottom): © John
Bigelow Taylor/Art Resource, NY; p. 7 (top): © California Historical Society, FN-32151; p. 7 (inset): © California
Historical Society, FN-23593; p. 8: © CORBIS; p. 9 (map): Courtesy of the Bancroft Library, University of
California, Berkeley; p. 9 (bottom): © Lake County Museum/CORBIS; pp. 10, 11, 19, 20, 22, 24, 29: © North
Wind/North Wind Picture Archives; p. 12: © Perkins/San Francisco Public Library; pp. 13, 14 (top & bottom), 31
(top): Courtesy of Katherine Watt and The Angel Island Association web site; p. 15: © Official U.S. Army
Photograph/SFC J. Gathings/San Francisco Public Library; pp. 17, 40: © National Library of Medicine; pp. 18, 23
(bottom), 30 (top), 43 (top & bottom): © The Granger Collection, New York; p. 21: © Hulton Archives/ Getty
Images, Inc.; p. 25 (top): © Bettman/CORBIS; pp. 23, 25 (bottom), 27 (left & right), 28, 30-31, 33, 34 (bottom),
39, 42: Courtesy of the Library of Congress; pp. 26, 37: © MPI/Getty; p. 32: Courtesy of the National Archives; p.
34 (top): San Francisco History Center, San Francisco Public Library; pp. 35, 41: Courtesy of California State Parks,
2006; p. 36: © California Historical Society, FN-18240; p. 44: © Philip Gould/CORBIS

All rights reserved.

No part of this publication may be reproduced, except in the case of quotation for articles or reviews, or stored in
any retrieval system, or transmitted in any form or by any means, electronic, mechanical, photocopying, recording, or
otherwise, without written permission from the publisher.

For information contact:
MONDO Publishing
980 Avenue of the Americas
New York, NY 10018

Visit our web site at http://www.mondopub.com

Printed in China

07 08 09 10 11   9 8 7 6 5 4 3 2 1

1-59034-808-7

Designed by Annette Cyr

Library of Congress Cataloging-in-Publication Data

Campbell, Wallis.
  Angel Island / by Wallis Campbell.
     p. cm.
  Includes index.
  ISBN 1-59034-808-7 (pbk.)
  1. Angel Island (Calif.)--History--Juvenile literature. 2. San Francisco
Bay Area (Calif.)--History--Juvenile literature. 3. Chinese
Americans--History--Juvenile literature. 4. Immigrants--United
States--History--Juvenile literature. 5. United States--Emigration and
immigration--History--Juvenile literature. 6. China--Emigration and
immigration--History--Juvenile literature. I. Title.
  F868.S156C36 2006
  979.4'62--dc22
                                            2005011316

Contents

Introduction

The Jewel of the Bay

San Francisco Bay in California is dotted with picturesque islands. Of the 11 major islands, one of them, Angel Island, is referred to as the "Jewel of the Bay." Covering 740 acres, today the hilly island is a state park, covered with grass and forests and dotted with campsites and trails. There are spectacular views of San Francisco, the Golden Gate Bridge, and the entire bay area. Part of the island's coastline is sheltered—visitors can go boating and enjoy the beach—but much of its coast is rough, and there are dangerously strong currents in the surrounding waters.

However, Angel Island is much more than a park. A sprinkling of buildings on its grounds is a clue to its rich history. The island has been everything from a Native American campground to a United States government missile base. But at the heart of its history is the Angel Island Immigration Station. From 1910 through 1940, this station was the main point where foreigners arriving by boat from routes through the Pacific Ocean would enter the United States.

Angel Island has been called the Ellis Island of the West. But unlike the European immigrants who passed through Ellis Island in New York Harbor, most people passing through Angel Island's doors were Asian. And, more strikingly, Angel Island ended up being essentially a prison for many immigrants—a detention center for people who were guilty only of being "different." Everything about the mainly Chinese immigrants seemed strange to people living in San Francisco—their skin color, clothing, customs, language. Many Chinese immigrants were held at Angel Island for weeks, months, or occasionally, years. Only then were they allowed into the United States—or, in many cases, sent back to a harsh life of poverty in China.

The story of Angel Island does not begin with the immigration station. Its location in San Francisco Bay made this a valuable piece of land, and just about everyone who came across the island wanted to claim it. During the course of its history, the island has been owned by three countries—Spain, Mexico, and the

United States. In addition to being the site of an immigration station, it has been a Native American campground, cattle ranch, missile base, and busy wartime military post. It was even once a quarantine station, where sick people arriving on ships could be kept until they recovered so they would not make others sick.

Angel Island's fascinating story begins thousands of years ago…with the arrival of the Miwoks.

Angel Island is located in San Francisco Bay, in Northern California.

Chapter 1
The Miwoks

Angel Island's known history begins about 5,000 years ago with the arrival of the Coastal Miwoks, a Native American tribe. The Miwoks were hunters and gatherers who lived on the mainland of what is today San Francisco, California.

Light, quick boats carried the Miwoks to the island where they established temporary camps. The island was full of wildlife. The surrounding waters were brimming with fish, and edible roots, berries, and plants grew wildly. It was a paradise for hunters and gatherers.

Some Miwoks lived in bark lodges like this one.

Miwok Men

Before going hunting, Miwok men spent time in hot houses, called sweat lodges, to sweat out their human smells. They also made deer heads to wear while hunting. These customs helped them surprise and catch their prey more easily.

The Miwoks made baskets like this one that they used during feasts.

Acorn granaries, or storage huts, where Miwoks stored acorns

Native Californian woman collecting fallen acorns

Miwok settlements were small so as to not use up the surrounding natural resources. The island provided plenty of food and other necessary supplies. Acorns from the island's many oak trees made up an important part of the Miwok diet. They ground the nutritious seeds into flour, which they then used to make bread and soup.

The island remained a quiet, peaceful place until 1769. That year, Europeans "discovered" this jewel in the bay.

Miwok Women

Miwok women collected lettuce and placed it near red-ant hills. When the ants walked on the leaves, they gave off a vinegar-like substance that the Miwoks used like salad dressing.

Chapter 2
The Spanish Period

In 1769, Spanish explorers, led by Gaspar de Portolá, sailed into the bay. However, it would be six more years until Europeans set foot on the island. In 1775, another Spanish explorer, Lieutenant Juan Manuel de Ayala, entered San Francisco Bay and set foot on the island that would become known as Angel Island. Ayala and his men raised the Spanish flag and named the land *Isla de Los Angeles* ("Island of the Angels" in Spanish).

The Spanish already held claim to land in North America. The area they called New Spain stretched from Mexico through what today is the Southwest region of the United States, including California. Ayala's sailing master, Jose de Canizares, explored the bay area, making detailed notes, sketches, and measurements—the first map of San Francisco Bay. During his explorations, Canizares received gifts of fish and nuts from the friendly Miwoks, who visited the Spanish ship and admired its rigging.

Mission Dolores, shown here in 1860, was built in San Francisco in 1791.
It was the sixth mission built by the Spanish in California.

Because this newly explored land held great promise, Spanish leaders built a mission—a religious settlement run by priests—in San Francisco. A major purpose of Mission Dolores was to strengthen Spain's hold on an area far from the Spanish capital in the New World, Mexico City. Miwoks were coaxed into farming the mission's land and caring for its cattle. In return they were fed and housed at the mission. However, they were also pressured to convert to Christianity and to become

Jose de Canizares's map of San Francisco Bay

more like Europeans. Little by little they gave up their native language, clothing, and customs. By the early 1800s, all Miwoks either lived at Mission Dolores or had resisted and fled the area. Less than 50 years after their first encounter with the Spanish, most Miwoks had died from diseases brought from Europe—smallpox in particular.

Mission Dolores, circa 1900-1910

In 1821, Mexico gained independence from Spain and took control of what is today California and parts of the southwestern United States. To prevent European powers like Britain and Russia from invading their northern border, Mexico strengthened its position by replacing the Spanish mission system with permanent settlements. The Mexican government handed out parcels of land to Mexicans so they would move north and settle in the area. One such Mexican was Antonio Maria Osio, who, in 1839, was granted Angel Island. Osio raised cattle on the island and sold beef in San Francisco for many years.

The Mexican government was also willing to give land to Americans living in the San Francisco area. However, it demanded that these locals become Mexican citizens first—something most Americans weren't willing to do. Instead, some Americans became squatters, living on unoccupied land in Texas and California without legal claim to it. In 1836, settlers living in present-day Texas won their independence from Mexico. By 1845, the United States had annexed Texas and set its sights on acquiring California.

A group of Mexican cowboys, called *vaqueros,* outside a mission in California in the 1800s

Mexican women making tortillas in the 1800s

Mexico, angry over the annexation of Texas, attacked United States troops on disputed land, and war began in 1846. But by 1848, Mexico had been defeated and had to give up two fifths of its territory to the United States, including present-day California, Utah, Nevada, and parts of New Mexico, Arizona, Colorado, and Wyoming. In return, the United States paid Mexico $15 million in war damages.

In 1848, after the Mexican War, Angel Island became a United States territory. After California became a state in 1850, Angel Island became part of California. At that time there were disputes about land ownership. Osio tried hard to keep his title to Angel Island and filed claim after claim. Finally, in 1860, Osio appealed to the United States Supreme Court, which ruled against him. Angel Island belonged to the United States.

Chapter 3
The United States Military

After California became a state in 1850, the United States decided to build two forts in the unprotected San Francisco Bay. One, Fort Point, was at the entrance to the bay; the other was on Alcatraz Island. The government then decided that Angel Island would be a good place for an army base, and in 1863, construction began on the base, called Camp Reynolds. The Civil War had begun two years earlier, and some feared that Confederate naval forces might threaten the bay area. Although completing the base became increasingly important as the war grew worse, much of Camp Reynolds wasn't finished until 1864, when the war was nearly over.

With the end of the Civil War, protecting the bay became less important, and most Army personnel left Angel Island. Camp Reynolds became a recruit depot— where new soldiers stayed before going to fight in the Indian Wars. These battles against various Native American tribes including the Nez Perce, Cheyenne, and Apache took place in the United States plains from about 1866 to the 1890s.

Camp Reynolds, Angel Island

The West Garrison, Fort McDowell, Cal.

Fort McDowell, Angel Island

During the 1870s and 1880s, the United States was mainly concerned with rebuilding a country torn apart by the Civil War. By 1889, however, focus returned to protecting the bay. In response, the government built a mine casemate, or storage area, on the island that could fire underwater torpedoes at enemy ships. In 1886, construction of three new gun batteries, or artillery stations, began on the island, before the United States declared war on Spain in 1898. However, the batteries weren't completed until 1902—too late to be of use during the Spanish-American war, which had ended in 1898.

As a result of this war, Spain lost most of its empire, including the Philippine Islands in the Pacific Ocean, which it ceded to the United States. Less than a year later, when the Philippine Islands rebelled against United States control, troops were once again based on Angel Island at Fort McDowell. United States army facilities on the island had been renamed in honor of Civil War hero Major General Irwin McDowell. For several years, the fort was an important base of operations during the Philippine-American War.

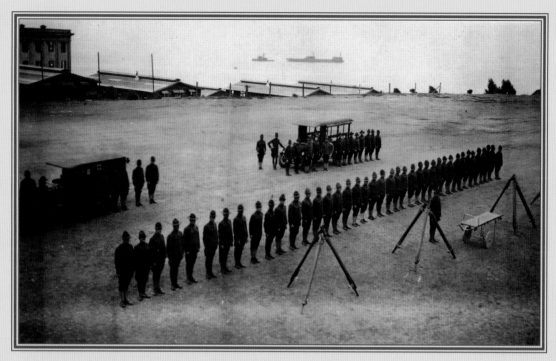

Soldiers on Angel Island during World War 1 in 1918

Throughout the twentieth century, a military presence existed on Angel Island. During World War I and World War II, the island was referred to as a "soldier factory," because recruits were constantly arriving and then quickly being sent off to battle. During both world wars, the island's Army post expanded. However, after World War II, the Army no longer considered Angel Island a good spot for a fort because of its isolation. They proposed the release of Fort McDowell to other uses.

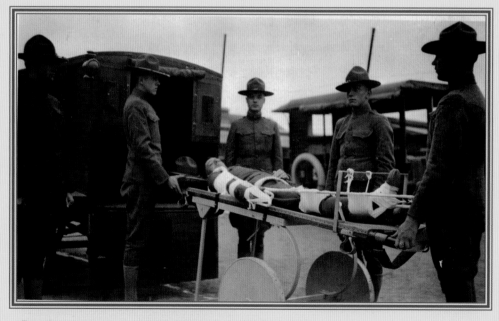

Bandage practice on Angel Island in 1918

Angel Island missile site in 1958. Pictured here are 4 of the 12 antiaircraft missiles that were stored here.

For about 10 years, Angel Island was quiet. Then, in 1954, as tensions with the former Soviet Union heightened, the Army looked to the island once again. An antiaircraft missile site was built and equipped to shoot down enemy airplanes. This missile site remained until 1962 when military presence on the island ended after more than a century.

Prisoners

During World War II, Japanese and German prisoners of war were held on Angel Island before being sent to a permanent camp. Because of its rough surrounding waters, the island was considered escape-proof!

Chapter 4
The Quarantine Station

In the late nineteenth and early twentieth centuries, before the discovery of penicillin, infectious diseases were a much greater threat than they are today. It wasn't unusual for ships arriving in the United States to be carrying travelers sick with the plague, smallpox, or cholera. To deal with this problem, the government decided to set aside part of Angel Island for a quarantine station in 1888. Because the island was isolated from the mainland, it was an ideal place to quarantine people carrying infectious diseases.

Chinese men arriving at Ayala (Hospital) Cove for quarantine

Immigrants at the quarantine station waiting for their luggage to be disinfected

The quarantine station opened in Ayala Cove (known then as Hospital Cove) in 1892. When a ship carrying sick passengers docked, passengers were first checked by a doctor. Then, once they had been examined, they were made to wash with special soap and put on clean overalls. Their clothing and baggage were taken away and disinfected. Passengers were forced to stay at the station for 14 days, and each morning the living areas were cleaned with chemicals and salt water. The ships were also disinfected.

In its early years of operation, the station didn't have enough water or housing for everyone passing through. More buildings were added over time, as well as pumps to bring in salt water. By the 1940s, improvements in medicine, such as penicillin, reduced the threat of infectious disease, and the quarantine period was shortened. Over the years, use of the quarantine station decreased. Its isolated location on Angel Island—the reason it was built there in the first place—made it expensive and inconvenient to run. In 1946, the quarantine service was moved to San Francisco, and eventually most of the station buildings on the island were destroyed.

Items to be disinfected were placed on carts and pulled into the disinfecting tubes on rails.

Chapter 5
Chinese Immigration and Prejudice

Chinese immigrants aboard a ship to San Francisco
in the early twentieth century

In many parts of the world, jobs and money were scarce. Often there wasn't enough to eat. In the mid-1800s, across the Pacific Ocean from San Francisco Bay, life in southern China was especially harsh. Most people living there were farmers. Natural disasters such as droughts, food shortages, and floods along with wars and violence, caused the area's economy to collapse. It became nearly impossible for Chinese farmers to make a living.

Around this same time, word came that gold had been discovered in California. Chinese men in droves, especially those from rural areas, left their families behind to seek their fortunes in the goldfields across the ocean. They thought they'd quickly strike it rich and be able to send money back home. The United States soon became known as *Gum Shan*—Gold Mountain.

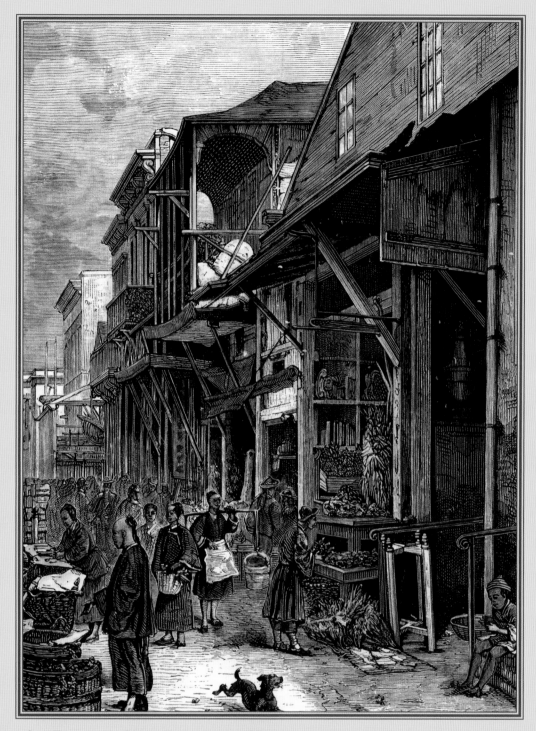

San Francisco's China Town in the 1870s

The area around San Francisco was the heart of the gold rush. Starting in 1849, many poor Chinese farmers arrived at the port and settled nearby, gravitating to the cheaper, poorer part of town, which soon became known as China Town (later Chinatown).

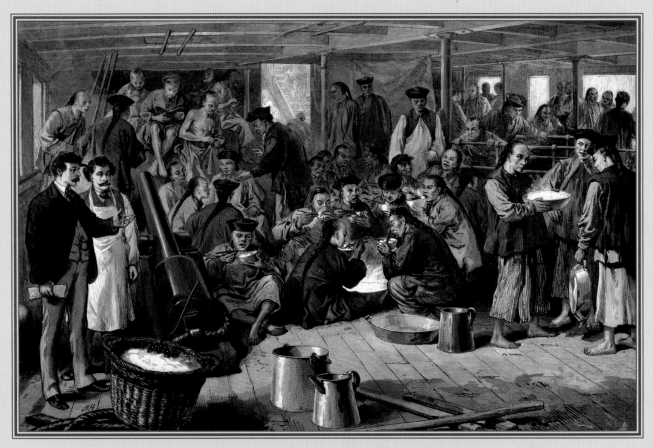

Chinese immigrants aboard a steamship bound for San Francisco in the 1870s

At first, Americans living in San Francisco didn't object to the flood of Chinese immigrants. There seemed to be plenty of gold to go around. However, as early as 1850, discrimination against the Chinese became more common. Once-abundant gold deposits soon began disappearing, and the ever increasing numbers of Chinese began to be seen as a threat to the American way of life. Competition over whatever gold remained led to the passage of the Foreign Miners' Tax Law. Passed by the California government in 1850, the law required foreign miners to pay a $20 per month mining tax.

This law didn't specifically target Chinese miners, but at the time most foreign miners were Chinese. For them, $20 was a lot of money. Most Chinese miners couldn't pay it, and many had no choice but to give up mining for gold. Those who continued trying to make a living by mining were increasingly forced out of gold-rich areas by American men who believed the Chinese were taking the gold that rightfully belonged to Americans. The Chinese had to resort to mining areas that had almost been completely stripped of gold by previous miners. With tiring effort, more gold could often be found—but usually not enough to live on.

Prejudice against the Chinese also meant they were not allowed to live in the nicest parts of the mining towns. These neighborhoods were reserved for long-time residents. So the Chinese survived by living in the worst areas. They were kept separate from Americans and often did not have clean water and were not allowed to go to public schools—services that were available to other taxpayers. In 1856, this anti-Chinese feeling led to violence. Some American miners went so far as to enter a Chinese community, attack the people, and destroy their homes and businesses.

Chinese panning for gold

Chinese working on the Central Pacific Railroad in the 1860s

Forced out of the gold fields, the Chinese turned to other, mostly lower-paying, jobs, such as working for the Central Pacific Railroad. They risked their lives laying tracks for the western section of the transcontinental railroad. They set explosives and made work tunnels under deep snow. Many lost their lives when heavy avalanches buried entire work camps.

Chinese immigrants were resourceful. They used skills learned in China to create new opportunities in California, such as cigar-making, doing laundry, shrimp and seaweed fishing, wine-making, and farming. However, the anti-Chinese feelings held by many Americans remained. The local government passed additional laws that seemed to be aimed at preventing these immigrants from succeeding at anything. For example, some Chinese caught shrimp, which they dried and shipped back to China where it was in demand. They were left alone until shrimp became a popular food in California. Suddenly shrimp fishing seemed like a good idea to local American fishermen, and the Chinese were once again seen as taking away the locals' livelihoods.

As a result, the government passed restrictions on the shrimp industry—requiring Chinese to buy special licenses, preventing them from using their own special fishing methods, limiting the number of pounds they could catch, and shortening the fishing season. These restrictions hurt the Chinese shrimp trade to China.

Chinese shrimp fishermen

The Chinese took whatever jobs they could find in order to survive. Thus they provided cheap labor and did work no other groups were willing to do. They built roads through dense forests and rugged mountains. They drained swamps and built dams. These difficult and dangerous jobs enabled the Chinese to make lives for themselves in the United States—but they were lives marked by prejudice and hardship.

Chinese doing other people's laundry

Chapter 6
Discrimination Worsens

A man named Denis Kearney riles up an anti-Chinese
mob in San Francisco in the late 1800s.

When the Civil War ended in 1865, the United States economy was weak. By
the 1870s, unemployment was at an all-time high in California. White workers
disliked the Chinese who, because they were willing to work for lower wages, were
thought to be taking jobs away from long-time residents. Community leaders
responded to these complaints by passing more local and statewide restrictions
against the Chinese.

For example, the Cubic Air Ordinance of 1870 made it illegal for anyone to rent rooms that had less than 500 cubic feet (14 cubic meters) of air per person. Because the Chinese often shared small rooms to save money, this law prohibited the only living arrangements many of them could afford. The Sidewalk Ordinance of 1870 outlawed the use of poles to carry bundles of laundry or vegetables on the sidewalk. Because these poles were the best way for Chinese workers to transport bundles, this law made it more difficult for them to run their businesses.

Cramped living arrangements of Chinese immigrants

Anger toward Chinese immigrants often turned into violence. Mobs stormed Chinese communities, stealing, killing, and burning. In Los Angeles in 1871, a mob of curious locals had gathered to gawk at the scene of a shooting between two Chinese. A white onlooker was accidentally shot and killed, and a riot broke out. Chinese property was robbed and burned, and 19 Chinese were killed. No one was punished for the loss of Chinese lives and property.

Chinese man carrying laundry. The Sidewalk Ordinance of 1870 outlawed using poles like this one to carry laundry.

CALIFORNIA. THE CHINESE AGITATION IN SAN FRANCISCO—A MEETING OF THE WORKINGMEN'S PARTY ON THE SAND LOTS.—From a Sketch by H. A. Rodgers. See Page 57.

A meeting of the Workingmen's Party in front of San Francisco's City Hall in 1879. This party, formed during bad economic times, was against Chinese immigrants who were thought to be undercutting wages.

The worsening United States economy and increasing violence in Chinese communities caused anti-Chinese feelings to grow stronger. No longer was discrimination against this group limited to California laws. In 1882, the United States Congress passed the nationwide Chinese Exclusion Act, which prevented Chinese laborers from entering the United States for a period of ten years. Just merchants, diplomats, students, teachers, and tourists would still be allowed to enter. Under this law, Chinese laborers already living in the United States were prevented from applying for citizenship. For the first time in United States history, a group of workers was denied entry solely on the basis of race. In addition, laborers already living and working in the country could not bring their wives over—so they had to decide whether to go back to their families in China or stay alone in this country to work and support them, and risk never seeing their families again.

Violence against the Chinese continued. In 1885, a Eureka, California council-man was accidentally shot and killed, and Chinese immigrants living in the area were accused of the crime. In the interest of public safety, local residents demanded that Chinese residents—whom locals believed were dangerous—be removed from town. These forced removals occurred in other California towns and counties, too, even when no violence had been committed by Chinese immigrants. This period became known as "the Driving Out."

Old newspaper cartoons about the Driving Out

Terrible living conditions in a Chinatown near Monterey, California

At about the same time, several fires broke out in Chinese communities. Some appeared to have been started on purpose. Three separate fires started in the city of San Jose at the same time, when city water tanks happened to be empty. In the town of Chico, a fire destroyed almost the entire Chinese community. The town's main fire hose had been suspiciously cut in four places, greatly hampering firefighters' ability to put out the fire.

The United States government was also making life miserable for Chinese immigrants. In 1888, Congress passed the Scott Act. It kept Chinese laborers (who had arrived in the country before the Exclusion Act was passed) from returning to the United States after leaving for a short time. This meant that men who had gone to China for a quick visit with their families, leaving their possessions and businesses in the United States, were not allowed back in.

As a result of the unfair laws and general prejudice, Chinese immigration to the United States dropped by about 40 percent from about 1880 to 1980. In 1892, passage of the Geary Act, which renewed the Exclusion Act for 10 more years, also allowed officials to arrest and send back to China any immigrants without papers showing that they lived here and had a legal right to do so. Not surprisingly, many Chinese did not have these papers. But still they came to America by the hundreds, hoping and searching for a better life. What they found often fell far short of their hopes and dreams.

Anti-Chinese rioters are kept back by fire hoses in Denver, Colorado, in 1880. Similar events were occurring in California around the same time.

Chapter 7
A New Immigration Station

Before 1910, immigrants arriving at the port of San Francisco by ship were held at a two-story shed while inspectors determined whether or not they would be allowed to enter the United States. Conditions there were so awful that local Chinatown community leaders complained to United States officials about them. More than once, inspectors visited the detention shed, and each time they found it cramped, crowded, and filthy. Still, for a time nothing was done to improve conditions for immigrants.

As a result of the failed inspections and the many complaints, United States government officials decided to

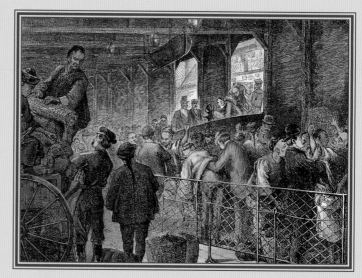

Chinese immigrants in San Francisco detention shed

After ships carrying immigrants docked at Angel Island, the immigrants would disembark and walk down the long pier to the new immigration station. Photo circa 1925.

build a new station, and Angel Island seemed the perfect place to build it. Like the immigration station Ellis Island in New York Harbor, this new station was to be a place where both the immigration process and quarantine could be handled.

The new Angel Island Immigration Station in 1918

In 1905, construction of the new station began in an area called China Cove, on the east side of Angel Island. The following year, however, while construction was underway, one of the most devastating earthquakes in history hit the area. The quake damaged part of the island, delaying construction of the new station. Another obstacle was the shortage of fresh water on the island, which would continue to be a problem even after a well was dug in later years. Then in 1908, 32 immigrants escaped from detention in San Francisco. Only three were recaptured, and local citizens were outraged. These escapes reinforced the need for the new station. Finally, on January 22, 1910, the Angel Island Immigration Station was officially opened.

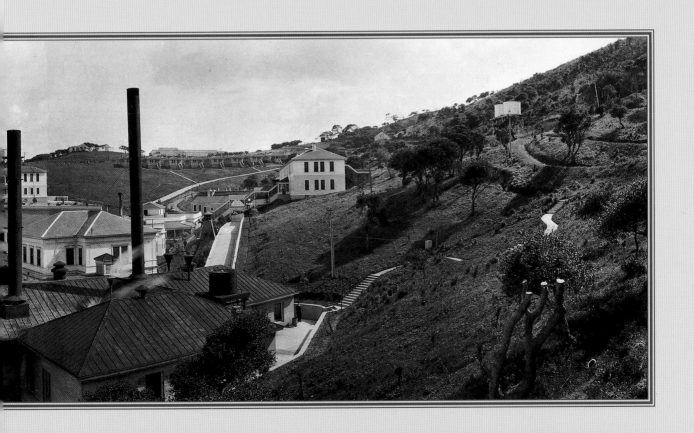

The purpose of the new station was to improve the immigration process by making it quicker and less upsetting. However, for the 30 years the station was in operation (1910–1940), it served also as a detention center. And those immigrants who were detained were mainly Chinese. Because of laws against the immigration of certain nationalities—especially the Chinese—many of the Asian people arriving at Angel Island had little chance of being allowed to enter the United States. For these individuals, a temporary stopover at the immigration station could turn into days, weeks, or months. And then, very often, they'd be sent back to China.

The typical Chinese immigrant's experience often went something like this. Upon arriving at the port of San Francisco by ship, officials checked the passengers' papers. Because of the Chinese Exclusion Act, only diplomats, merchants and their families, students, teachers, and tourists from China were allowed off the ship—and then only if their papers were in order. Passengers were then taken to the Angel Island station by boat.

Asian immigrants arriving at the Angel Island Immigration Station in 1911

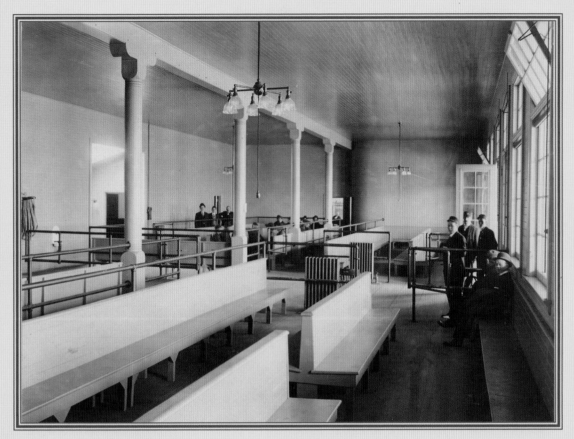

The examination room at the immigration station

    In addition to the large number of Chinese, immigrants also arrived at the Angel Island station from Japan, the Philippines, Russia, Armenia, Mexico, Central and South America, Korea, India, and Europe. At the immigration station, a person's treatment often depended on his or her nationality. Asians were separated from Caucasians and other races. Then Chinese were separated from Japanese and other Asian immigrants. Although treated worse than Europeans, Japanese who passed through the station didn't suffer as much as the Chinese. Once the Chinese were separated from everyone else, the men and women were split up—including husbands and wives. They weren't allowed to talk to or see each other until after admission was approved. Children under 12 stayed with their mothers.

Immigrants were then taken to the island's hospital for an examination. Because the Chinese were unfamiliar with American culture and medical procedures, they found the examination extremely embarrassing. They were required to remove all of their clothing, which, because the Chinese never exposed themselves like that, made them ashamed.

Immigrants playing baseball on Angel Island in 1930

Those who passed the medical examination went to live in island housing while waiting to find out if their applications for entry had been accepted. Immigrant housing was cramped and uncomfortable. Doors were locked from the outside, and guards made sure no one escaped. Metal bunks were stacked two or three high in rooms that were often dirty and overcrowded. The food was neither tasty nor nutritious.

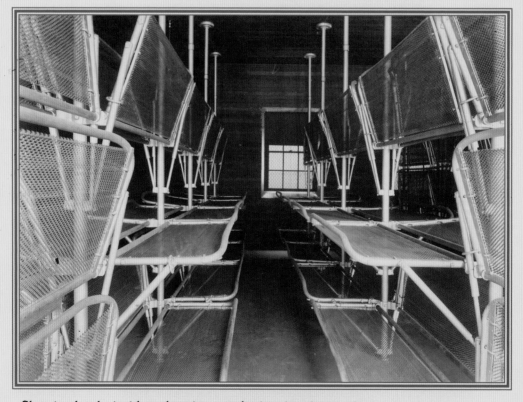

Sleeping bunks inside a dormitory at the immigration station

Chinese women taking a walk on the grounds of the immigration station, circa 1925

If they wanted clean clothes, the immigrants—now held as detainees—had to wash their garments in sinks and hang them inside to dry. Their days were spent waiting, worrying about being sent back to China, playing games, and reading. Men who had money gambled, and many women knitted and sewed. The detainees were treated much like prisoners. For short periods each day, the men were allowed into an exercise yard. Groups of women and children were allowed to take walks on the grounds.

Riots

Riots sometimes took place because of the dreadful food. One uprising, in 1925, was so out of control that troops from Fort McDowell were called in to restore order.

Katherine Maurer with detainees in the late 1920s

The Chinese Chamber of Commerce in San Francisco, which had objected to the station even before it was built because of its remote location, was upset at the conditions. An important part of the immigration process was having witnesses (who had to be current, legitimate United States citizens) tell about an immigrant's character. Chinese leaders believed it would be too difficult for witnesses to get out to the island.

Although some praised the new station as "delightfully located" and "modern," many others agreed with local Chinese leaders. The Acting Commissioner of Immigration for San Francisco noted that the station was unsatisfactory because of errors in construction and poor maintenance. But requests to move the station to the mainland were still ignored.

Some help did come to the Chinese detainees, however, in the person of Katherine Maurer, a Methodist deaconess. For 28 years she provided them with toothbrushes, toothpaste, combs, and sewing material. She got hold of toys and books for the children. She taught immigrants English and helped those who were finally admitted into the United States to find jobs. The Chinese called her *Kuan Yin*, which was the name of the Chinese goddess of mercy. People from the San Francisco Chinese YMCA, the Hebrew Immigrant Aid Society, and the American Baptist Home Mission Society also made regular visits to the island to provide services and support.

An organization that provided much needed help to the Chinese was the Angel Island Liberty Association. It was created in the 1920s by Chinese men and boys being held at the station. The association made formal complaints about unacceptable conditions to the immigration staff. For example, toilet paper and soap, though regularly given to detainees from other countries, weren't provided to the Chinese. After the association's formal complaint, however, the Chinese finally were given these and other basic items. But still problems remained.

Chinese immigrants being taught English in California, circa 1885

Many Chinese immigrants held at Angel Island applied for entry to the United States by claiming citizenship through birth or descent, which meant they had a parent who was already a citizen. The problem, however, was that most immigrants didn't have the legal paperwork to prove their claims. As a result, many Chinese sought a way around the unfair immigration laws. For example, a Chinese man who was a United States citizen would visit his family in China and then, after returning to the States, would lie and say that a child of his was born back in China. Because the law stated that the children of United States citizens were citizens as well, by reporting a false birth, the Chinese man would create an opening, which he could then sell.

Men who entered the United States through these purchased openings were called *paper sons*. They arrived with new names and families. Sellers provided paper sons with coaching papers containing all the necessary facts about their new family, home life, and native village. The paper sons memorized these facts before their interviews with immigration officials.

Coaching papers could also be purchased through the Angel Island Liberty Association. Chinese citizens who worked at the station smuggled them in. Some of the money raised from selling these papers was then used to buy items that would improve life at the station.

Coaching Papers

The questioning of immigrants was so harsh that sometimes even lawful immigrants failed to pass or would resort to coaching papers to memorize information and details about their own relatives.

In re
Jung Fun,
Minor son resident Chinese merchant.

--oOo--

State of California,)
City and County of San Francisco.)SS.

Jung Fung, being first duly sworn upon oath, doth depose and say:-

That affiant is a merchant lawfully domiciled and resident in the City and County of San Francisco, State of California, and engaged in business therein as a member of the firm of Shing Fat & Co., which said firm is engaged in buying and selling and dealing in merchandise at a fixed place of business, towit:-No. 677 Jackson Street, in the said City and County of San Francisco.

That affiant has been a merchant a member of the said firm for more than one year last past, and during the said time has engaged in the performance of no manual labor except such as is necessary in the conduct of his business as such merchant.

That affiant makes this affidavit in order to identify Jung Fun, whose photograph is hereto attached, as his son. That the said JungFun is the lawful minor son of affiant. That he is now in China, but that he is lawfully entitled to admission into the United States, and that he is now about to come to the United States to take up his residence therein with affiant.

Jung 雪達 Fung

Subscribed and sworn to before me,
this...16.day of .... A. D. 1911.

Thomas S Barnes
Notary Public,
In and for the City and County of
San Francisco, State of California.

The man pictured became a paper son by taking on the identity of Jung Fung — the son of a legal San Francisco merchant — in order to be allowed into California, in 1911.

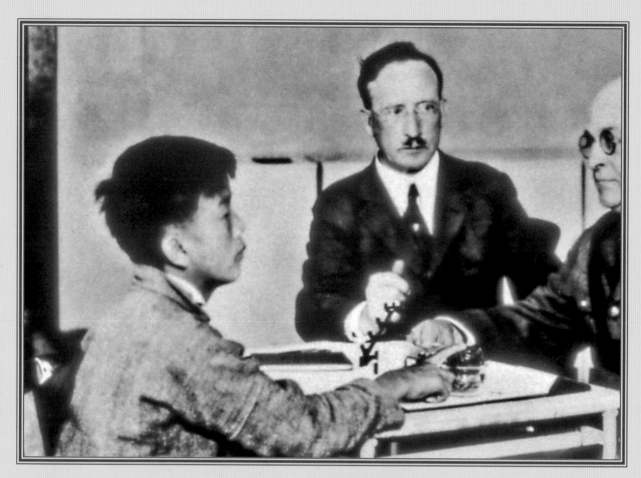

A Chinese immigrant being interviewed at the immigration station

Typically, interviews were led by an inspector, with a secretary to record what was said and an interpreter to translate for the immigrants and their witnesses. Immigrants usually waited a long time at the station before their interviews finally took place. When the station first opened, the delays could stretch for months, although by the 1920s, the wait was down to two or three weeks.

The interview process was complicated. First, the immigrant was questioned alone. Then the immigrant's witnesses (usually family or friends) were questioned to check his or her answers. Because the purpose of the interview was to determine whether or not immigrants were indeed related to the United States citizens they claimed as family, the questions asked were extremely specific. For example, *How many steps are there to the front door of so-and-so's house?* Or, *What material is the flooring of so-and-so's bedroom made of?* If the answers given by both an immigrant and his or her witnesses didn't match, the immigrant could be sent back home.

Some inspectors were fair and kind, but others were unfair and frightening. Immigrants complained that the detailed questions were meant to confuse them and their witnesses on purpose. Because of these complaints, a committee made up of San Francisco merchants led an inquiry into the interviewing process at Angel Island. They found that some boys as young as eight were being asked their grandmother's maiden name and the names of people living in their neighborhood—things very few children would know. The committee declared the questions to be too hard. But still the same difficult interview process continued.

Two immigration officers processing papers for one Asian man and several Asian women at the Angel Island Immigration station, circa 1925

Here, in their own words, is what some of the Chinese immigrants thought about the interview process.

In our days, we didn't have electricity, just kerosene lamps. And you know, a kerosene lamp's a moveable object. So what was I supposed to say if they asked where was the lamp kept? My father might have said the middle of the table or the end of the table. I didn't know. I couldn't understand why they were asking such questions.

—Mr. Poon, age 18 in 1927

Professional portrait of young Chinese woman in San Francisco

They asked me so much, I broke out in a sweat. Sometimes they would try to trip you: 'Your husband said such-and-such and now you say this?' But the answer was out already and it was too late to take it back, so I couldn't do anything about it. . . .

—Mrs. Chin, age 19 in 1913

From *Island: Poetry and History of Chinese Immigrants on Angel Island, 1910-1940,* by Him Mark Lai, Genny Lim, and Judy Yung, HOC DOI, 1980.

Immigrants who did not pass the exam could appeal, or argue, to be allowed in, but examiners' decisions were rarely reversed. About 60 to 80 percent of all appeals were turned down. When an immigrant appealed, it meant another waiting period—anywhere from two to six months, and in rare cases as long as two years.

Chinese immigrants outside the hospital at the immigration station, circa 1910

Chinese immigrant children in San Francisco's Chinatown in the early 1900s

Conclusion
The Angel Island Legacy

Surprisingly, despite the difficult entrance exam, a majority of Chinese applicants were allowed into the United States. In 1923, for instance, out of 5,009 applicants questioned, inspectors passed 4,806 of them. Although it might not seem as if many people were turned away, this rejection rate of some 200 out of 5,000 people was much higher than the rejection rate at Ellis Island, which was only about two percent. However, Chinese waiting at the Angel Island Station for days or weeks on end had no way of knowing that most immigrants were let in.

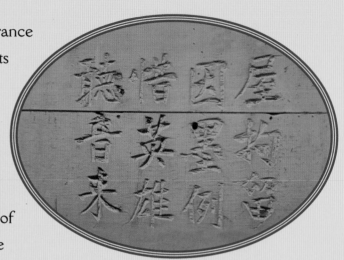

This poem, which is in Chinese, was carved on the wooden walls of the immigration station's detention center.

In 1940, the United States government decided to close the Angel Island Immigration Station. In 1943, the Chinese Exclusion Act was repealed. World War II was being fought, and China was now the United States' ally. By 1963, most of Angel Island had been turned into a park. One day, in 1970, a park ranger noticed some Chinese writing carved into the station's walls. They were poems — brushed

Women at Angel Island

There were far fewer women held at Angel Island, and very few of them could read or write. None of the poems collected were written by women. But because the Immigration Station Administration Building, where the women then stayed, burned down, it's possible that some were written by women, too.

with ink or carved into the station building's walls—revealing the Chinese immigrants' anger, fear, loneliness, and sadness. Although the government wasn't interested in the poems, the Asian American community became involved. With the help of the Angel Island Immigration Station Foundation, they persuaded the government to save the historical barracks building. It has since become a museum that recreates one of the dormitories and features some of the poems that were carved there. Its many exhibits educate the public about the Chinese experience in America, especially on the island.

Instead of remaining a citizen of China, I

willingly became an ox.

I intended to come to America to earn a

living.

The Western styled buildings are lofty; but I

have not the luck to live in them.

How was anyone to know that my dwelling

place would be a prison?

✦

There are tens of thousands of poems

on these walls.

They are all cries of complaint

and sadness.

The day I am rid of this prison and

attain success,

I must remember that this chapter

once existed . . .

✦

From *Island: Poetry and History of Chinese Immigrants on Angel Island, 1910-1940,* by Him Mark Lai, Genny Lim, and Judy Young, University of Washington Press, 1980.

Glossary

annex　　　　　To add an area of land to an existing area or territory

antiaircraft　　Designed to defend against air attacks

artillery　　　Weapons

barracks　　　Military or prison living areas

coaching papers　Documents studied by paper sons that included information about their new identity. Paper sons studied these papers in order to convince immigration officers they were who they claimed to be.

detainees　　　People who are held somewhere against their will, despite the fact that they are not criminals

discrimination　Act of treating some people better than others without a fair reason

dispute　　　　Disagreement

gun battery　　Group of guns and other weapons

mine casemate　Armored storage area from which torpedoes can be fired

mission	Religious settlement run by priests
paper sons	Men who bought and adopted a false identity—as sons of United States citizens—in order to be allowed into the country
penicillin	Medicine that cures infections
picturesque	Beautiful, pleasant to look at
prejudice	Dislike of a person or persons for no good reason, but often due to their race or culture
quarantine	When the sick are separated from healthy people to prevent a disease from spreading
recruits	New soldiers
squatters	People who live on land that they don't own or rent
transcontinental	Going across, or spanning, an entire continent

Index